Coming To

Coming To

Poems by J.R. Solonche

David Robert Books

© 2022 by J.R. Solonche

Published by David Robert Books
P.O. Box 541106
Cincinnati, OH 45254-1106

ISBN: 9781625494085

Poetry Editor: Kevin Walzer
Business Editor: Lori Jareo

Visit us on the web at www.davidrobertbooks.com

Books by J.R. Solonche

The Five Notebooks of Zhao Li

Selected Poems 2002 – 2021

Years Later

The Dust

A Guide of the Perplexed

The Moon Is the Capital of the World

For All I Know

The Time of Your Life

Enjoy Yourself

Piano Music

The Porch Poems

The Jewish Dancing Master

In a Public Place

If You Should See Me Walking on the Road

To Say the Least

True Enough

In Short Order

Tomorrow, Today, and Yesterday

Invisible

Won't Be Long

I, Emily Dickinson & Other Found Poems

Heart's Content

The Black Birch

Beautiful Day

Peach Girl: Poems for a Chinese Daughter (with Joan I. Siegel)

Table of Contents

Coming To..11
The Snow Was So..12
My Neighbor...13
Posted...14
Sometimes When I Awaken In The Morning....................15
Greenhouse...16
Beggar..17
The Poetry Reviewer Wanted To Know..........................18
March...20
Sonnet..21
Reading Su Tung-P'o..22
The Snow Melts...23
The Snow Melts...24
The Snow Melts...25
Sonnet..26
The Little Left..27
Corroboration..28
Blue Skies Again..29
Someday...30
The Wind..32
Poetry To The Rescue Again...33
Scarament Sacrament...34
Enough...35
Never Rude To Intrude With Gratitude...........................36
Two Swans..37
Kill Skill..38
Tired Old Tire..39
The Wild Cherry Tree...40
Frivolity..41
How It's Done..42
Calling..43
Degrees...44
Hawk Talk...45

Anxiety	46
On A Wire	47
The Rules	48
The Telephone	49
Stone Wall	50
When I Hear	51
My Neighbor	52
Sentimentality	53
The Blessing For Caressing While Undressing	54
Already	55
Sprung Spring	56
I Heard Whispering	57
First Fly Of The Season	58
Cornell	59
Rain	60
Swimming Lesson	61
Ambition	62
Second	63
The Clouds Climb Up And Over	64
I Just Forgot What	65
Today The Sky	66
This Morning	67
An Unlikely Story Is Likelier	68
The Hawk	69
Galactic Action	70
Miss And Hit	71
Nothing Today	72
Jeo	73
One Way Or The Other	74
Enough	75
Remembrance	76
What They Say	77
The Big Old Ash Tree	79
Motive	80
The Widow Thaler	81
Going Back	82
Too Many Poets	83

Words	84
Impertinence	85
Overheard In A Bar	86
The Grievances Of Levitation	87
I Need A Woman	88
The Bee	90
April Ninth	91
Knowledge	92
Depths	93
Schoolhouse	94
Small Song	95
Nonexistence	96
Freedom	97
Happiness	98
Stone's Story	99
Cloudy Day	100
Poem	101
Grackles	102
Matchmaker	103
Songlet	104

COMING TO

is not the same as going to

which, because

it requires the first step,

is so much harder.

No, coming to is the easy part.

It means you're almost there.

THE SNOW WAS SO

The snow was so

completely deep,

so deeply complete,

the world so winsome

completely in white,

I thought it was making

itself a virgin again.

MY NEIGHBOR

My neighbor has apple trees.
They are old.

I have never seen them with apples,
so they must be old for a long time.

He should cut them down.
Old dry apple wood makes warm fires.

POSTED

On my walk today, I saw
new *Private Property* signs
posted on the trees. No man
should own woods. No matter
how dark they are, no matter
how deep they are, no matter
where they are, no man
should own woods, I say.

SOMETIMES WHEN I AWAKEN IN THE MORNING

Sometimes when I awaken in the morning,

I don't know who I am, for it seems

I leave my identity in the dream.

Sometimes when I awaken still knowing

who I am, I don't know where I am,

for it seems I leave my whereabouts in the dream.

Sometimes when I awaken knowing who and where

I am, I don't know what the world is as it waits

for me, whoever I am, wherever we are.

GREENHOUSE

I wonder if they know
(as much as chlorophyll
can know anything
other than the sweetness
of the energy of sunlight
and rain on its tongue)
that as they perish into
winter's dead sleep, these
inside, these rich relations,
will live on, all wide awake
and wide-eyed, glowing in
the warm glow of their
winter palace. I wonder if
they knew, would they then
demand their own entry there,
or like a revolution's mob,
break every pane with bricks
and cobblestones?

BEGGAR

I gave a dollar to a beggar
sitting on the sidewalk.
As soon as I did, I saw
that all the people in the city
were dressed in rags, and
all of us were wearing plastic
bags on our feet, and all of us
smelled of the world, some
more, some less, and all of us
had our hand out, and all of us
were past shame. I saw that
all of us were long past shame.

THE POETRY REVIEWER WANTED TO KNOW

The poetry reviewer wanted
 to know what poets will do
when the outrage is over. "Will
they go back to writing about
flowers and moons?" he asked.
I can only speak for myself, but
I have never stopped writing
about flowers and moons.
The flowers have always been
there in rows around the outrage,
and the moons have always
overhung the outrage like the heads
of celestial roses. Yes, flowers
everywhere: chrysanthemums
and irises, pansies and marigolds,
sunflowers and azaleas, clematis
and even a black satin petunia.

Yes, moons, too, mostly our own
in all her phases, from none to full
and back again, but also the moons
of Saturn and Jupiter, Mars. Uranus,
and Neptune, and even the one that
doesn't exist, the moon that Venus
doesn't have. Why is an astronomical
mystery. I'm a poet, not a polemicist.
Poor Venus, poor lonely Venus,
the only one moonless (Outrageous!),
poor lonely, lonely goddess.

MARCH

The sun

shines softly.

The snow

melts slowly.

A lone crow

wipes its small

wings on the wide

white of the lake.

SONNET

What stopped you?

What stopped you from seeing it?

Wasn't it was right there in front of you?

What stopped you from hearing it?

Wasn't it right there behind you?

What stopped you from believing it?

Wasn't it right there in the heart of your mind?

What stopped you from doing it?

Wasn't it right there in your hands?

Was it the future that stopped you?

Was it the past that stopped you?

Did they both stop you?

Didn't they both stop you, the future and the past?

Yes, didn't it take both the future and the past to stop you?

READING SU TUNG-P'O

There he goes.

He's off again.

Headed south.

Or headed back north.

One wife gone.

Then another.

Finally a lover.

Experts at farewell,

the poems always leave gracefully,

but how awkward at arrivals

they are, how awkward and sad.

THE SNOW MELTS

The snow melts.

The stone wall

is exposed

as are the trees

that fell and lie face

down beside the stone wall,

as though huddled for warmth.

THE SNOW MELTS

The snow melts.
The icy water rushes down
to the road ditch
and through the long culvert,
which was the plan all along.

THE SNOW MELTS

The snow melts.

Without their cold white blossoms,

the trees are dead again.

But the crow in the maple knows better.

"Do not despair," it says.

"I hear the green heartbeat of your leaves.

Do not despair.

I will be back soon."

SONNET

Isn't it a good thing you weren't there?

What would you have done?

Would you have stamped your foot?

Would you have made a fist in the air?

Isn't it good, isn't it good you weren't there?

Wouldn't you have ruined everything?

Wouldn't they have only stared at you?

Wouldn't they have only brought you to tears?

Isn't it a very good thing you weren't there?

Wouldn't their laughter have followed you out?

Wouldn't hers have been the loudest and longest of all?

Wouldn't you have only felt only despair?

Wouldn't you have been so small, so small?

Isn't it a damn good thing you weren't about?

THE LITTLE LEFT

The little left of snow

is still snow where

it fell weeks ago,

these white shadows

stubborn in the tree shade.

CORROBORATION

Amazing how still

the bourbon in

the glass remains

given how fast

the universe

is accelerating

from itself, Ammons.

BLUE SKIES AGAIN

I look, Ammons,
but I do not leap.
It is just as blue
down here even
though you cannot
see it for the green.

SOMEDAY

Someday, I want to see
a limousine, a silver limousine,
a long limousine, pull up into
the driveway. Someday, I want
to see a star, a silver star, step
out, the door opened by a chauffeur
in a silver uniform, and walk up
to the front door. Someday,
I want to hear a star knock on
the front door and ask, "Why
does your door have no bell?"
Someday, I want to say, "Because
I am expecting you." Someday,
I want to say, "Please come in,"
and she, the silver she with
the silver stars in her hair and
with the silver moon pinned
to her silver gown, would come

in, then turn to send her

silver limousine away.

THE WIND

The wind was so
insistently fierce,
so merciless,
it must have been
intent on stripping
the beech tree of
its leaves at the behest
of the jealous oaks
who had already lost
their own for weeks.

POETRY TO THE RESCUE AGAIN

Even if what
we hear is only
the clip-clop,
clip-clop of
coconuts cut
in half, it's still
the cavalry,
right Ammons?

SCARAMENT SACRAMENT

It was in a poem

about going to church.

It was the most

frightening

typographical

error I ever saw.

ENOUGH

Yes, enough
for now.

Now for
enough.

NEVER RUDE TO INTRUDE WITH GRATITUDE

It's always welcome.

No matter what.

No matter when.

No matter where.

No matter how it's done.

It's never rude to intrude

with gratitude,

for gratitude is sunlight,

and sunlight is never rude.

TWO SWANS

Two swans glide

on the lake in pure silence,

one the white shadow of the other.

I know one is male and one female,

but not knowing enough about swans,

I do not know which is female and which is male.

I want to believe the one leading the other around

by the nose is the female.

For political reasons.

KILL SKILL

The hawk has it.

The shark has it.

The cheetah has it.

But this fucking spider has it in spades.

TIRED OLD TIRE

Tired old tire,

why are you still here?

I thought I had seen the last of you

on the right rear wheel of my Subaru wagon.

But no, here you are on your last legs,

well past your last legs, leaning against

the wood shed.

The trash men wouldn't take you.

A brief reprieve, old Goodyear.

I'll soon get rid of you.

If not now, next year.

THE WILD CHERRY TREE

The wild cherry tree

has its chance

to catch the sun

in its basket of branches,

and does but will be the last

to let the sun go free and horizonly west.

FRIVOLITY

They look so frivolous.

I'm nervous.

This is serious.

This life is serious business.

These turtles on that log

down there

should not look so frivolous.

There's more to life

than the sun, isn't there?

HOW IT'S DONE

Two mourning doves sit
on the wire between the pole
and the house.
They look uncomfortable.
They look like they're going to fall off.
But they are determined to see it through.
They are good at how it's done.

CALLING

I was called.
Who isn't?
I was called and answered,
"He's not here."
I was called and answered,
"Call back later."
I was called and answered,
"Call me in a few years
when I know you and
why you're calling me."
She never did.

DEGREES

They grow by degrees

in the right degrees,

the forsythia, the snow drops,

the crocus, the freeze

forgotten as if it never happened,

as if the snow had never been,

except for the rain

that welcomes it back again as water,

as son, as daughter.

HAWK TALK

A pair of hawks

call to one another.

One is loud and raucous,

insistently demanding,

the other softer,

more demure,

using whatever the word

for *darling* is in hawk.

ANXIETY

It is more low than high,
a simmer of anxiety,
the white noise of it,
the natural backdrop
to a tragedy or a farce.

ON A WIRE

On a wire,

a bird is counting to three.

Then to two.

Then to three again.

Then again to two.

It's a simple code

which so far no

mate has cracked.

THE RULES

They're not written,

of course, but

hardly unspoken.

I hear them all day long

in every language

of the woods, of the swamp,

of the lake, of the sky.

What a joy to hear

the singing of the spoken rules.

THE TELEPHONE

The telephone rings.

It isn't mine.

It's my neighbor's.

I hope he answers it.

It sounds important.

STONE WALL

Hard to believe
I built that damn thing.
Hard to believe I put stone on stone on
stone until there were enough
stones to make what anyone
would have to agree was a wall.
But I didn't do it to make good neighbors.
I did it because I felt like doing it.
I needed to satisfy an urge.
I needed to write a stone poem for a change
instead one writ in sand.
Or water.

WHEN I HEAR

When I hear
the mourning
dove mourning,
I stop what I am
doing to listen.
Then I go back
to what I'm doing
more mournfully.

MY NEIGHBOR

My neighbor
is burning something.
I think they are leaves.
It doesn't matter
what he is burning.
The smoke is heavy
and dark. It rises over
the outcropping
between our houses,
a visible stench almost
as foul as a rumor.

SENTIMENTALITY

The woman in the car
with the window open
next to me at the red light
listening to my second
favorite Bach cantata was
almost beautiful. I almost
wept. Cynicism is not
black and white.

THE BLESSING FOR CARESSING WHILE UNDRESSING

They didn't think

of that one,

those Levites who

came up with the 613.

Or did they?

ALREADY

Already the grasses are ready.

There's no holding them back.

They throw aside the leaves

of last year with ease. They rise up,

their backs straight as rails,

to announce, "We're back!"

SPRUNG SPRING

I remember melting,

but I don't

remember being ice.

I HEARD WHISPERING

I heard whispering
behind me and thought
students were whispering
about me, but it turned out
to be just a few dry leaves
talking behind my back
behind my back.

FIRST FLY OF THE SEASON

Hey there, little guy.

Welcome to the world of people.

You'll like it here.

You look right at home already,

sitting on the table,

rubbing your hands together.

All you have to do now

is learn how to salivate.

CORNELL

After the extraordinarily
beautiful young woman
walked past me in the other
direction, a young man came
along. "If you hurry, you might
catch up with her," I said as
I pointed to the extraordinarily
beautiful young woman just
disappearing between buildings.
Was I being impertinent?
Not if it paid off.

RAIN

It is raining, so I listen
to the rain on the roof.
The rain is talking
to the roof, not to me.
Nevertheless, I cannot
help eavesdropping.

SWIMMING LESSON

I push the pen

into the deep end,

so deep, it can't see

to the bottom.

AMBITION

After a day of doing
nearly nothing,

I vowed to get nearer
next time.

SECOND

Each homeless man has his own.
I like the one on Second the best.
He moved from Third because
he couldn't compete with the one
already there. He has no teeth.
He's saving up for dentures. Or
so he says. I like his smile. I like
his lies. His lies are also smiles.
He reminds me of me a little.
Of course, I'm very generous.

THE CLOUDS CLIMB UP AND OVER

The clouds climb up and over

the western hills hitching a ride

on the wind as though they were

the western hills with an itch

to be the hills of the east.

I JUST FORGOT WHAT

I just forgot what
I just remembered.
That's all right. Soon,
I will just remember
what I just forgot.
Perhaps they'll even
be the one I mean.

TODAY THE SKY

Today the sky
was so cloudlessly
blue, it was the blunt
end of bland, but still
it gestured earthward
grander than any grand
gesture down here.

THIS MORNING

This morning I nearly
tripped coming down
the stairs. Do I have that
right? No. I tripped. I nearly
fell. I must be more careful.
I don't want to live the rest
of my life downstairs on
the first floor. I write better
on the second floor, up there,
that much closer to the moon.

AN UNLIKELY STORY IS LIKELIER

An unlikely story is likelier
than likely. The beginning
is for beginners, the middle for
the mid-life crises, the ending
for waiting on the end to end.

THE HAWK

The hawk was at just
the right longitude,
at just the right latitude,
at just the right altitude
to whistle with just
the right attitude.

GALACTIC ACTION

From planet to solar system to galaxy doesn't take as long as you may think. Just a hop, a skip, and a jump. But galaxy to universe is another matter, one that requires a lot more space to tell.

MISS AND HIT

The spider missed
twice, then a third
time unbelievably
before she hit a
perfect bull's-eye
of silk on the apex
of the milkweed.

NOTHING TODAY

Nothing today that
wasn't also yesterday,
that will not also be
tomorrow, but let us wait
and see what yesterday
will bring back from store,
what tomorrow has in store.

JEO

A poet friend of mine called
me *Jeo* in an email. It's the
best typo I've ever seen.
I'm going to use it as my name,
especially after looking it up
in the *Urban Dictionary* and
finding out it means "Jeo a guy
who loves you for you....i person
that will take his time with you.
Hes not that pretty but hes sweet,
caring, kind hearted, athletic,
funny, chill, and can also be freaky
He a person that is responsible
and respectful. *(JEO)-can treat
you as a queen*" Aw-shucks.

ONE WAY OR THE OTHER

There must be more
than two ways,
the one the one way
and the one the other way.
Two ways seems so unfair,
a coin toss all that's needed
to settle the affair,
a simple heads or tails
to choose who wins, who loses.
No, there must be more I'm sure.

ENOUGH

The sun and the clouds
have managed to stay away
from one another enough
for the swamp to warm up
enough for the turtles to
sunbathe long enough on
the log long enough for all five.

REMEMBRANCE

I forgot to close
the garden's deer
fence door, so a gust
of wind remembered
and closed it for me.

WHAT THEY SAY

My wife says I get sweeter
when I drink too much.

My daughter says I get
more aggressive when I drink too much.

My friend Jim says I get funnier
when I drink too much.

Does this mean I'm aggressively sweet
and funny when I drink too much?

Or that I'm comically aggressive
and sweet when I drink too much?

Or that I'm sweetly funny
and aggressive when I drink too much?

Or that I'm aggressively funny
and sweet when I drink too much?

Or that I'm sweetly aggressive
and funny when I drink too much?

Yes, I think that's what they mean.
That's what they all mean.

THE BIG OLD ASH TREE

The big old ash tree
is the granny of the yard.
She guards them all.
All who seek her protection,
she protects. All who seek
her shade, she shades,
All who seek her shelter,
she shelters. All who seek
her loving embrace, she
lovingly embraces. See?
There's my chair.

MOTIVE

I hate my neighbor's rooster.
I would like to kill it.
Mind you, this has nothing
to do with envy.

THE WIDOW THALER

I saw the widow Thaler today.
She was cycling with my neighbor,
Tom. She looked good. She lost weight.
She grew out her hair. It was also lighter
brown. She was wearing jeans. They
were tight. They looked really good.
She looked good. I was jealous of Tom.
But I understand. She can't keep a secret.
That was what she said, and I understand.
She doesn't have to keep a secret now.
Tom isn't married. I could have though.
I could have kept a secret. I could have
kept it for both of us. I'm a poet. But
I don't have to either now. Tom isn't
married. She looks good. She looks good.

GOING BACK

I don't believe in going back.
I don't believe in going back
to the childhood home. I don't
believe in going back to the old
neighborhood. I don't believe
in going back to an old poem.
Going back is an admission of
defeat. Or an admission of something
else. And I don't believe in admissions.

TOO MANY POETS

Too many poets
tell me I remind
them of them.
Two would have
been enough. One
man. One woman.

WORDS

What's the matter with words

that they must matter so much?

The monks know, but they don't say.

IMPERTINENCE

Permanence is
impermanent.

Impermanence is
permanent.

How impertinent.

OVERHEARD IN A BAR

First man:

"So how's your love life?"

Second man:

"Not so hot, but my hate life is better than ever."

THE GRIEVANCES OF LEVITATION

When I read that, Ammons,

my hair stood on end. Finally,

it was what hair is supposed

to do when you're reading a poem

but never does, which is why

I've stolen it from you.

I NEED A WOMAN

Do you know what a woman is?
I used to know what a woman is,
but I have forgotten since then.

Now I know only that I need one.
Have you ever needed something real bad,
but you didn't know what?

Isn't that sad? Isn't that so sad?
That's how I am about a woman.
No, I don't know what a woman

is. I know only that I need one real bad.
I know what a woman is not.
I know a woman is not a man.

I know a woman is not a cat.

I know a woman is not a canary.

I know a woman is not a convertible.

I know a woman is not a fairy.

But, shit, I don't know what a woman is.

I know only that I need one.

I know a woman is not a bottle of bourbon.

I know a woman is not a villanelle.

What a woman is not I know very well.

 I know only that I need one like hell.

He lies who says he knows what a woman

is. He knows only that he needs one.

THE BEE

The bee met me
at the mountain laurel,
softly feeling out
the flowers' undersides
too small for it, but
there were no hard
feelings on either side.

APRIL NINTH

On the day before

the wild cherry blooms,

the honey bees dream

their last dream of Paradise.

KNOWLEDGE

We do not know what

a breeze needs for it

to be a wind, so

we look to the trees

and the leaves they let go.

DEPTHS

At the shallow end

of the lake, the snapper

heaves her heaviness

across the road to lay her eggs.

Who knows how many times

she has done this. Who knows

how many more she will.

These are the depths forbidden to us.

SCHOOLHOUSE

It was a schoolhouse.

Now it is their house.

There was a bell in the tower.

The bell called the children to school.

Now there are beds in the tower.

The beds call the children to dream.

It was the house of learning.

They learned to read and to write.

They learned to add and subtract.

Now it is the house of relearning.

They learn to live and to die.

They learn to add and subtract again.

SMALL SONG

All songs are small,
Ammons. That is why
they are songs.
Shall we rather say
small symphony?

NONEXISTENCE

Someday my nonexistence

will be how I exist.

Please feel free

to put two and two together.

FREEDOM

What was once an ash tree

now is a stump in the grass.

It may or may not remember

having been the lord of the lawn,

but the lesser trees do not care,

for either way, they are freer.

HAPPINESS

Why do the daffodils,
erect, up to their waists
in the water of the vase
look so much happier than
they did in the ground?
Should I ask my friend
Jim the philosopher, or
should I ask my friend
Emil, the biologist?

STONE'S STORY

If you've heard one,
you've heard them all.
True, but I'm still
waiting to hear one.

CLOUDY DAY

Although you may
think they are,
a cloudy day
and a day of clouds
are not the same.
A cloudy day
includes the mind.

POEM

I've never read a bad
poem called "Poem."
I know that's what
poets call their poems
when they can't come
up with a real title.
They should do it
more often, though,
because, like I said,
you'll never read a
bad poem called "Poem."

GRACKLES

The grackles break
through the sky's cracks
in a single dark mass,
the afternoon wearing
a sparkling black mask.

MATCHMAKER

A white butterfly

flutters across the grass

looking to mate.

Another white butterfly

flutters identically

through the garden's weeds

behind me looking to mate.

"Over here. Over here," I call

to the first hoping to strike

the flame with my flinty voice.

SONGLET

Let song be
the key.

Words are
optional.

Hum the tune
if you must.

But in key.
But in time.

And for just
as long as song.

About the Author

J.R. Solonche is the author of 24 books of poetry and coauthor of another. He has been nominated for the National Book Award and twice-nominated for the Pulitzer Prize. He lives in the Hudson Valley.